THE
MORE
THE
MERRIER

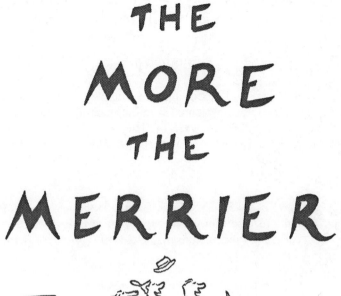

CARTOONS
BY
MICHAEL MASLIN

A FIRESIDE BOOK
PUBLISHED BY SIMON & SCHUSTER, INC.
NEW YORK

Of the 110 drawings in this collection, 56 originally appeared in *The New Yorker* and were copyrighted © in the years 1979, 1980, 1981, 1982, 1983, 1984, 1985, and 1986 by The New Yorker Magazine, Inc. Grateful acknowledgment is made to *The New Yorker* for permission to reprint.

The cartoons on pages 34, 35, 37, 48, 50, 52, 53, 58, 60, 63, 65, 67, 75, 85, 90, and 107 are reprinted courtesy of *Mother Jones* magazine. Grateful acknowledgment is made to *Mother Jones* for permission to reprint.

A Fireside Book
Published by Simon & Schuster, Inc.
Simon & Schuster Building
Rockefeller Center
1230 Avenue of the Americas
New York, New York 10020
FIRESIDE and colophon are registered trademarks of
Simon & Schuster, Inc.
Manufactured in the United States of America
1 3 5 7 9 10 8 6 4 2
Library of Congress Cataloging in Publication Data
Maslin, Michael.
The more the merrier.
"A Fireside book."
1. American wit and humor, Pictorial.
I. Title.
NC1429.M4247A4   1987   741.5'973   86-27876
ISBN: 0-671-63535-2

FOR ALBERTA AND AL

"We'll take it."

"It was right where you left it—under the table."

THE BUB CLUB

"I love it when you hug the curb."

"Nothing but French Provincial all these years, then—whammo! The Country Look."

*"What does fall mean to Richard C. Dottledge, of Pinestay, Pennsylvania?
It means leaves—and plenty of them."*

"Thursdays he swashbuckles."

"Bob up and down."

The Lost Serenaders

"Whoosh."

"Sir, a Mr. Krueller, of the real world. Are you in?"

"Bonbon?"

"Don't just sit there—recline!"

"We won't be eating for quite awhile—Marie's still wrestling with the soufflé."

Stuck in the Muck in Full Regalia

"She only dives with a drum roll."

"*You're cute—but you're trespassing.*"

"*I love to watch the morning light play across your face.*"

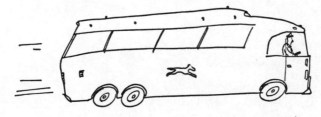

"We're at the home of Jim and Mindy Marks, who are about to discover that their utility bill has gone sky-high. Let's watch."

THINK RINK

"It's a blender, Morton. We've got to stop living in the past."

SLEDDING IN BED WITH FRANNY AND FRED

"*A dozen kisses—chocolate.*"

"It's for you."

"This is my favorite part of our summer vacation—when you lean into the wind."

THE PLOT THICKENS

"Mr. Kenny here will attempt to resolve our differences."

"Monique, wait! I've changed my mind. I'll have the pistachio after all."

"*Apparently, there is going to be a disqualification.*"

"There's no substitute for good conversation."

A GREAT CUP OF COFFEE

"Honey, I'm home! Hey, wait a second—I'm not married."

"That will be Williams with your Twinkie."

"Esteemed if I do, esteemed if I don't."

"*Don't let that innocent face fool you—it's just a facade.*"

"*I'm offering you a chance to be somebody.*"

"We'll continue clickety-clack down the track immediately following this delay."

"Hello, dear, or is it goodbye?"

"This isn't Quebec."

"How much would you pay for all the secrets of the universe? Wait, don't answer yet. You also get this six-quart covered combination spaghetti pot and clam steamer. _Now_ how much would you pay?"

"Mrs. Rhinebat, I presume."

First Big Snowfall of the Season Takes Albert Cranfield by Surprise

"*Extremely fresh salads, Sir. Indeed, our tomatoes just came in.*"

"Well it certainly looks like a castle to me."

"*I now show you this popular dance from the sixties,
and ask you if you've ever seen it before.*"

"*Just between the two of us, there are three of us.*"

"At a thousand dollars a plate, you really don't think I'd forget the plate."

"All of this hinges on whether I'm dreaming."

"Of course they may look entirely different on Mr. Santuzzi."

"*Professor Brunner is fascinated with his own mind.*"

"This is Mr. Feldon—the next of kin."

"How can you be so down, down, down, when everyone else is so up, up, up?"

"Bob, I'm a Pleistocene man, I roamed the earth about two hundred thousand years ago, and I liked to work with stone."

"When he leaves, I'm in charge."

"Mom, Dad—this is Lois."

"I'll rise, but I'm damned well not going to shine."

"You're not going out of *this* house wearing *that* smile."

"We now have 570 snowballs to your 525. I just hope we never have to use them."

"I don't get it. They run, but they're not chasing anything."

"Duncan Brindly of Appleman, New Jersey—come on down."

"The more Humbert changes, the more Humbert stays the same."

"I find you up in the middle of the winter and you tell me nothing's wrong?"

"Surf's up."

"You know what they're saying all over town, don't you?
They're saying you're <u>always</u> out of butter pecan."

"*The Supreme Court! Well, this is a surprise.*"

"*Good morning! This is Dick Howard on your radio.*"

"Oh, Mr. Erdle—not just raked, but stacked too!"

"Speak."

"That's for me to know and for you to piece together."

"Ken, Martha—please don't feel you have to entertain me."

"Meet the candidate. Meet the candidate's pug-dog."

The More the Merrier

". . . and so it was, and so it was to be what it was to have been, and had what it was to have had, had it had what it was to be what it had to have been . . ."

"I'm the Fruit Fritter, he's the Coconut Snowball, and she's the Boston Cupcake."

"Well, this is a coincidence. I too am headed for Barbados."

"*And bless this fresh-roasted coffee. It has rich,
full-bodied flavor, __and__ it's decaffeinated.*"

"Pterodactyls? No, we haven't had them in ages."

"*Six hundred-and-four dollars?—I'll have to put the yeast back.*"

*"It was the Dewey Decimal System that brought them together
and the Dewey Decimal System that broke them apart."*

"*And a side order of fries.*"

"Life is a cabaret."

"Will there be anything else, sir?"

"Stay."

"You don't know me, but I know your Crêpe Suzettes."

"Shake. Sit. Speak."

"Yes, Washington slept here—but that was a long time ago."

"This is everything a vacation should be. You and I, sand and saltwater in our hair, tanning beside the deep blue sea. Laughter, soft music, and the scent of suntan lotion in the breeze. And hot dogs with mustard on sale right over there."

"Mitchell—herd of four."

"This room is half the rate of our others,
but you have to share it with Mr. Frickstone."

"Orson, look. A little Russian submarine."

"*In this corner, a man prone to costly and lengthy litigation.*"

"It's Mr. Bochild, from upstairs, wanting to know when in blue blazes you're going to go out and build your snowman."

"If these figures are correct, the last doughnut is yours."

"You and your embezzling."

"Dave, wait—it's me, Alex Donnerfelt."

"I'm sorry, Danny, but that's the way it is.
Life—_even_ life under the microscope—is sometimes unfair."

"Murray, when you have a moment, I could use a fresh fifty-dollar bill."

"*As you walk among these ancient creatures, try imagining yourself clad only in a little fur shift.*"

"Bill, come inside before there's trouble."

"Lights! Cameras! Christmas!"

"It's a parade day."

"That doggy in the window is four hundred and twenty-six dollars."

"I must ask you something, Miss Begett. Did you try the tortoni?"

"You were sensational."